T0194459

THE GROWTH OF
AXIOM

SUSAN M. COOK

authorHOUSE®

AuthorHouse™
1663 Liberty Drive
Bloomington, IN 47403
www.authorhouse.com
Phone: 1 (800) 839-8640

Published by AuthorHouse 05/30/2020

ISBN: 978-1-7283-6339-4 (sc)
ISBN: 978-1-7283-6338-7 (e)

Print information available on the last page.

This book is dedicated to all who have taken the time to read it. I would like to thank the person who inspired me to write this book Mr. Brother George Fewquay, of Miami, Florida. I also would like to thank my family and friends for all the patience they have showed to me, as I figure out my path in life. After years and years of not understanding what my purpose in life was, I finally figured it out. I exist to be a blessing to others, which in turn bestows an abundance of blessings in my life. All of this is said out of respect for why I wrote this book, and to also capture and challenge my readers to take in account their actions upon others, and start to think about how what we all do impacts others. In old sayings we all know, "Walk a mile in my shoes", or "Put yourself in someone else's shoes", or just plain old "What goes around comes around", or like someone once said, "Things recycle. Hopefully we work on being careful how we treat others." This book was written with you in mind, so you can have the comfort of knowing someone thought about the very thing most do not, or might be too afraid to start a conversation about. As many of these experiences may be to hurt us, but the lesson and strength we gain from them can sometimes renew your ability to push through anything life has to throw at you. My greatest dedication goes to my mother, who taught me so much in life. She was self taught, by reading books and working with word puzzles, and for those who knew her, can attest to the long scrabble game nights, with whomever was up for the challenge. I love and miss your with all my heart.

In memory of one of the greatest parent in the world, who is my mother. It was her courage as a woman that set the model before me to become the woman that I am today. I stand nowhere close in her shoes, but strive to step into them day by day, by loving and helping others.

I Love You Mama,

Susan

"May Songbirds forever watch over you Mother"

The Growth of Axiom is based on the writer's
guiding principles that helped the writer
overcome a lot of hardship and learn through
the value of the connection of relationships.

THE GROWTH
OF
AXIOM

Susan M. Cook

Editor of this book and of (W2W) Woman2Woman
support groups and social events, hopefully, this
book helps someone better understand how to move
through a very complex world with much more ease.

Contents

Understanding the Order of
Birth and Its Impact on My Life

I am number seven of eight children to my parents. I was not able to understand my place in my family. I will start by saying, first, I was born of six children, who had already claimed their spot in the family, and five of the six were girls, and one boy child. I believe another boy was longed for, and along came my youngest brother four and half years after my birth. I never felt jealous, but I always felt I was not supposed to happen at the time I did. I surely had one of the most amazing mothers one could ever imagine. However, I believe, because I was not born at the expected time, this may have had some barren down on how, I was viewed in the family. This made difficult to find direction from ages 13 through early 20"s.

1

I learned to better understand my mother and family, and why things happened the way they did, through analyzing and understanding regardless of my place in the family. I believe my mother understood before she left this world, as she started to respect me as an adult in a different way, letting me know, she never had to worry about me.

Down through the years, I analyzed, prayed, and waited in life, until I understood; now I understand that the birth of my new understanding came out of the power of love and learning independence.

Lesson: Self Preservation was added to my tool box of life early from these experiences.

2

When Taboos Got a Grip and How I Overcame Them

It took me, until I was an adult to define a traumatic event. My first experience with this was when I was about 13 and a trusted individual, defiled my innocence as a teenager. I am not blaming or shaming here, as we are not free until we are all free, as I once saw on a license plate. My point here is to bring out my definition of trauma and its effects on me. This person never acknowledged it, and I never brought it to their attention, as they were under the influence of alcohol at the time, and I always used this reason as an excuse not to face it. This individual touched me inappropriately and it did not feel right as now I see that this was traumatic for me. This event, was cut off, because of a knocked on the door, as I answered it with a look of disbelief, as to what just happened, before the knock on the door took place. In just that Instance I was violated. I felt scared and alone, because when this happened to someone else I knew, this person was not believed ("as back in the day you just didn't talk about stuff like that"), and I threw it off, but never felt it was OK. This was yet another experience that taught me to be guarded and lose trust in men in particular. Again, this almost happened again by, individual I trusted, but they just felt guilty and did not follow through. I was so glad I was able to talk this person down, because this would have damaged me for life. After these horrific experiences, many experiences, involving men or boys happened in my life, that caused me to feel unsafe, fearful, and characteristics such as feeling inadequate became the norm for me, and I went into fright mode when faced with difficult situations involving boys and men. However, at different times in my life, I was able to be a beacon of light for one of my perpetrators, and this individual saw me in a different light, as well as held a hand of protection over me when it seemed necessary. It is strange to me how involvement in people can have many twist, and yet I have learned to choose the high road in dealing with agreements, I make with men. I learned to do this by becoming accountable for my own actions and letting God and the universe judge what happens next. However, if and when, I gained advantage over such events, I still did not try to pull down my perpetrators, but more so learned to lift those up who meant me no good. Also, I learned that I became the Victor. And the enemy really did become my foot stool, as these people had to face me in a different light, without me ever disregarding them as a human being, as all involved may not have learned the necessary tools to get through a very complex world. Please understand I am not dismissing the violation of a girl or woman here, and will respond appropriately, to harm meant to hurt young girls and women.

Lesson: Teachable lessons come through relationship building in the most peculiar form.

3

Learning through the Lives of Babes

Unexpectedly, I became pregnant at the age of 17. Not that it could not be expected by this time, and I was real familiar with the process. I had my first boyfriend at an early age. I wanted to be grown and date him, plus he was cute, had his own place, a car, and had weed. Not that I was a weed head, but I was a teenager in the 80's when MF was real popular. However, this individual did not work out. I met someone else and became a young mother not soon after meeting this individual. My daughter came out of this relationship, and she is my Angel. My daughter showed me how to love, feel compassion, and how to express my emotions, as growing up; this was not done much during this era of my life and seemed hard for people to express love, and how they felt on any topic in life. The one individual who has always supported me, has been my daughter, and at times she has been the one to lift my head up, when I was down, and motivate me to return to school to get my Master's Degree in Social Work, as well as helped me work through tuff relationships. She also, at times, pointed out my imperfections to help improve me, when she didn't know she was doing this. Life lessons were also transitioned through my daughter as it was through her that I learned about the difference in people, and how we all give and take from one another's culture. It's not even half bad, that through the hands of time, my daughter played the mother role and helped me pass my statics class in college. As I walked through the door after school and she said, "Mom, how you did on your exam today?" I held my head down, because she put so much into me getting it, but my brain could only hold so much. Well I passed with a "C", and she said, "But, Mom…", and we shared in a laugh about it. I said all this to let it be known, it does not matter the age of a person to learn a good lesson in life.

Lesson: Age is truly only a number and stay open to learn, learn, and learn again. I did not coin this saying, but it is so true. Maturity came for me, when I accepted the truth, whether I thought I had the answers or not. Remember you can learn something from age 0-100, the truth lies in the eyes and innocence of a child.

4

I Didn't Ask To Be Here, but Why I Believe I Exist

Often, I heard people say I didn't ask to be here, I never knew what to do with this, when I heard people say it. I do remember my mother's rationale for me and my sibling attempting to say this, the re-precaution, for this was, she made us all listen to Shirley Caesar "No Charge." Especially, the part "for the nine months I carried you, doctor you, prayed for you, no charge." Crazy as it may seem this too changed my life. As I look back, I realize one reason I believe I was born, is that I have been blessed to understand relationship, even at the cost of having to bounce back from some. I believe my gift to connect to lives is, so important to me, because I understand the importance of relationship building in everyday interactions with people. I personally often do this by sharing a smile. And I will tell you why a smile is so important in building relationships, and changing hearts. True story, I was headed one day to the mall. My spirit was not in a good place, and my head was down, as I walked into the double doors of the mall. A lady was coming out the door the same time I as entering it. She held the door for me, smiled at me, and at that point I thanked her. Her response after that blew me away and made my day. She said one simple word, "Pleasure" in an English-speaking tone with a smile, as if holding the door for me did something special for her, which in turn made me lift my head up and feel special, after going through a difficult time. This one good gesture made me feel so good, I added this to my life daily ritual, to offer a smile as much as possible to everyone that cross my path.

Lesson: I was told that an old African Saying not sure, but it goes like this, – you never know who you're smiling at; you could be smiling at your mother. For me this woman's smile made me lift my head up and appreciate if nothing else what a smile could do, and in that moment, she and I connected for life, whether she remembered it or not. This too was able to be added to my tool box of life, as a smile always gets me through tuff times. This life lesson taught me the wonderful reason, as to why I exist, to keep paying it forward like this woman did for me, with what one might think is the smallest thing, but for me her good gesture of (holding the door for me, while smiling), has taken me far in life, for me it mattered, on this day in particular.

5

You Can't Be What You Is To Save Your Soul. Coined by: A Religious Predecessor

This comes to mind when I think of how people try to use so many ways to rationalize, how they cope with not being accountable for their own actions. I often hear people make all kinds of excuses for things they know they need to change in their lives, or they try to live up to someone else's expectations, of who they think they should be. This can often appears artificial. Trust me I understand the concept of "*fake it till you make it*", but in the sense, that people often work way too hard on giving a care about what someone thinks, or feels about them. I have learned that until you value you, no one else will. Raising the value of you is often a lift to remembering one simple thing, and that is to love yourself and others. No matter, the situation we can all find a way to love self and share love and be creative in our thinking, so that we move through life as much as possible without hurting someone to the point their mental psyche has been disturbed.

Lesson: Learn to be real and find your truth. It is a lot closer to you than you know.

6

A Mother's Love

As I travel back in time, I can best define a mother's love through the love I was given by my mother, and the love I shared with my own daughter. I'll first talk about what a mother's love is to me. I was able to identify this early in life as it was exhibited to me in many forms. For as far as I can remember it was important for my mother to make sure her children eat well, had clothes, and plenty toys. I always saw her in the kitchen cooking and baking to satisfy the soul, and trust she did just that, as everyone who knew her, remember the fried pies she used to make. One of the best lessons I learned from my mother was when she said, "You can't tell me anything about my children, because I know them better than anyone else." Now that takes a real mom to know this, because back in the day, people would beat your children for anything they thought they did wrong. In raising my daughter with a religious background, reminds me a lot of the olden days when everyone, put a whipping on your back side. Well I was not one of those mothers, who gave out free licks at my child's expense. I taught my daughter well before she left home how to behave at least to the best of my ability. I used to say to her, "dead in the eye no lie." This meant you are now forced to tell me the truth. I believe my daughter learned from this to be honest, and that my expectations for her were to tell the truth. She also, did not have the concern of worrying about, someone other than her parent, hitting her up the stream to Easter Sunday, as well as damaging her emotional state as a young child because everyone knew, her mother, didn't allow this, and It was made plain, if my child was wrong, I would not take up for her, if she was indeed wrong, but I'll be dang it, if people, made my child's behind the sounding board for their personal pain. This built a great alliance among three generations, because of what my mother taught me, and through this, I was able to add this concept to my parenting skills, while at the same time protect my child.

Lesson: Listen to your children from birth to adult hood, and know them better that anyone else. Trust that you put the right thing in them as you build a loving wholesome trusting relationship bonded from a Mother's Love.

7

Why We Need a Moral Compass to Guide

I write this piece thinking about the world as a whole, and how from the beginning of time man as felt remorseful for their dirty deeds, convictions for the wrong committed on another or just refuse to believe that we may not get the answer we want. Often, we are told early in life to believe in God and he can do "ANTHING." This same approach was what I used as a guide for me, as to how I lived my life, raised my daughter and got in and out of relationships. I am not sure, as to if God would want such a strong expectation put on him, or if mankind has to figure out how things work before, God steps in and handles it for us. I believe how we treat one another is linked to an energy source in the universe, and what goes around truly comes around.

There is more than likely a higher being guiding us all. I believe this is in the form of "LOVE" and people deny it, are unsure what it is, and throw it around mindlessly. To love and share love is one of the greatest gifts, and love transitions across nations can change minds and build the greatest relationships. I believe love is that base for how we figure out a lot of answers in life, plus this takes the idea that God can do "Anything" away from our first line of consciousness, and makes it less questionable about what God can indeed do, or is willing to do. I came to this realization after spending years in the religious world, and hearing what is called, *"The Word of God"* seven days a week and twice on Sundays. A lot of this type of emphasis was put on God, maybe because people like the pie in the sky idea, and don't realize we have a personal purpose to fulfill. My assumption is when we look at how we came to learn something, and how this learning helped to shape us into who we are today (by way of such relationships with, parents teacher and peers etc.), it possibly makes us afraid to see things in a different light, as we are often afraid to challenge, or don't realize the need to challenge such beliefs that may have come out of these types of close relationship. Question is it these fears that make it difficult to face, who we have become today? For me, I started to do the very thing I was told not to do. Question my own religious views. I have yet to find anyone that can show me the imbalance, or reasoning in the belief that God can do "ANYTHING". When I look out into the world and see countries fighting in the name of God, and when looking right in my own countries' backyard, and see little children taking advantage of, and being victimized through sexual assault, before they can even understand what happened to them, and on the other hand, yes Sister, did testify last Sunday that she got healed of Cancer. It is these imbalances that make me question that in fact if the God can do "anything". I say this with no disrespect. I do believe that something out in the universe sacrificed, so much for the world to be what it is today. As I mentioned above in some of my life lessons. I do however, understand that it seems maybe, that people need a moral compass to guide and something to give credence to, and most never think about questioning what they learned in their own religious world, and how this may have impacted their lives presently, or probably forgot the sermon, as soon as they heard it, even though so much is attached and guided by the "Word." And how people have their own understanding of it. For example, the religious message that's often taught is such things as, a man that finds a wife finds a good thing. I cannot tell you how many weddings I have been in throughout my life. I mean the whole nine yards; limousines, wedding cakes, long dresses and all, but none of this made these marriages last. What happened to looking out and finding a wife, or what God put together let no man set asunder, come on, all these vows are broken every day. Awwh I know what your thinking maybe, God didn't put those together. See it's this type of thinking that keeps us separated and not open to loving and understanding of one another in knowing everyone's situation s unique to them. And because we would have to look at a lot of marriages before we can judge it this way. Let's look at the divorce rates and see if we can question that same question. Also, look at when a woman goes to her spiritual leader, about an abusive husband. She is often told to honor her marriage, as she continues to suffer at the hands of her perpetrator. It is these type of conditioned situations that are appear questionable. I am again am always open to learning how things got started. This was so hard to ever question something that has such a big place in society, and for me it was like, I had been lied to all my life. You know, like the time they told me there was no Santa. That stuff, really hurt a five-year-old child, but the cookie was bitten off and everything, so give me a break y'all, I may have been bamboozled.

Lesson: People are taught how to view the world early in life and they pick up on environmental external forces that predict their lives as well, however through ongoing building of relationships, I believe we all will get closer to finding out the validity of what God can, or is willing to do. I do however believe to make the world run better, we all have individual work to do, and if coupled with someone, couples work. I call it, I do my work, you do your work, and together we do the work to make a thing work. I would like to say thank you for reading this section it was very hard to write this, as even I don't have a clear understanding of what God can or is willing to do. (Continue to Pray for Me).

8

Don't Walk Under That Ladder, Crack That Glass Mirror or Walk across a Black Cat

S ay Amen if this resonant with you, if it does, you just told your age. Relax just kidding Loves, if you read this much of this book, I already appreciate your openness and understanding of the writer. Well I'll begin, I remember G Lady, without letting you know what the heck this meant, would say old sayings that stuck or maybe her own superstitions. I just knew if G Lady, said it, then it's got to be true. Seeing it from a practical approach G Lady, was teaching a lesson, but why she didn't just say, don't walk under the ladder, or you know "Bear", I walked under the ladder as a kid, and got hit in the head with a screwdriver, or something to this effect, because I was so mis-conskrewed about the ladder thing.

Let's not talk about the crack a glass mirror 7 years of bad luck deal. Rationale for this was it true? My thinking was, G Lady, meant don't break my damn mirror or the wrath of G Lady, gone be on you for about seven long years.

In actuality, it's said it was an old Roman saying that your luck renewed itself in seven years, whoosh, sweat popped off my face every time I broke one. Even with this you were able to in an indirect way build a relationship with whomever your G Lady was, based on a superficial belief she had. Y'all better not tell her it didn't hold no weight to this stuff. And the don't cross a black cat still scares me, and I know nothing happened a million times I passed a black cat. Just wanted to lighten the load of this one.

Lesson: Listen to your (Special G Lady), and embrace if for what it is.

9

When Daddy Don't Come Home

This one is very difficult to talk about, but if it helps someone on the journey of life, so be it. May 18, 1980, at the age of 17 years old, I lost someone close to me who, was killed near my place of residence, just a few months before I became a young mother. I remember a close relative yelling up the stairs into my bedroom, to come down and help get Heart out of the car. I was hung-over from handing out with friends in the hood the night before. It was about 4am in the morning, as I stumbled down the stairs and ran outside. I was not thinking about anything, but trying to wrap my head around what was taking place. I thought I was dreaming, as I looked at Heart, lay lifelessly in his new green and white Cadillac.

Another relative and I tried to pry the doors open to the car, while at the same time yelling, "Heart", but got no response. The ambulance had already been called, but not yet arrived. A well-known neighbor came out and pried the door open, and said, Heart was not sleep. He's been shot…he's dead." I started to cry and excitably say to Angel, why you not crying, Hearts dead?" Another neighbor, who was, Angle's friend said, "Angel is in shock." I did not know what in shock meant, plus I was still hungover. As the ambulance arrived my family started showing up yelling and screaming, and one of relatives as the EMT's put Heart's lifeless body in the ambulance, yelled out, "Get your hands off him! He ain't dead!" She was in shock as well. Who knew the man that helped pry the door open and I were in conflict over a misunderstanding with someone in his family, yet he was the one that was able to help my family with some type of rationale as to what was happening, but what the neighbors, were not able to relieve me of was the lift, I got from knowing, boy, I'm not glad Heart's dead, but this was the day the fighting stopped. Angel used to say live by the gun you die by the gun. She could not in many instances, save herself from the abuse, but sometimes life has a certain way of stopping things. Don't get me wrong I miss and love my Heart, who was a great provider, but the other side to him was led by standards of entitlement and abuse and from this, power and control came out of such behavior. Another side I miss is that Heart did what he could to help his family, even though his addiction was much more powerful. Detectives found out within a week who the perpetrator was, however this person did not win either. I guess it can be said there were no winner's in this situation. Heart used to take me to school every morning and now that was gone from me.

Lesson: Love they neighbor as you love thyself. If it were not for the neighbors on that day supporting my family, I don't know if my family and I would have made it through this as we did, and the fact Angel told her children to forgive the person that took Heart away from the family.

10

Boys Can Do This but Girls Can't

Growing up with mostly sisters and few brothers in the household, I witnessed a lot of double standards. The duties of the girls in the family were a routine activity of dishwashing for the week, until the cycle went through to the next girl, living in the house. This next thing, I'm about to say may have been my first-time experiencing disparities among the sexes. My brother's job in the household was to take out the trash, and I can only remember it being one can of trash and maybe a small one in the bathroom, and their other chore was to mop the kitchen floor, and I don't remember if they even swept it first, or if that was done for them too. What I do remember is that it felt unfair. This same type of injustices can be found in the male/female culture in society. Why I say this because early on, we learn that a boy is not supposed to cry, girls are tomboys if they climb trees, and even your clothes and toys are picked out for you according to your assigned sex. Assigned duties remained that way in my life up until now. How this became a blessing in disguise is that I have been able to build relationships through, this division. This made me look at how girls and women have been treated early in life, starting by looking at my own household. This also helped me look at how I started to view my brothers through this experience. My brothers learned to take on a new responsibility of caring for their sisters and helped provide at needed times, however disparities never got addressed during that era of time. There will probably always be disparities among the sexes, but I learned to look for more than the assigned label in people and what that produces, to get to know the better part of them, with hopes this sets the tone for a conversation around the impact of those differences.

Lesson: Building relationships among male family members can enhance the greatest experiences in one's life, and this taught me how to identify fairness in a situation, look at it for what is during a particular time, and later in life how to have a conversation, around such differences. Lesson received.

11

The Educated Mind

Only if I knew, is there a time in your life where you thought this, well I know I did many times. During my elementary school years, I did not know to appreciate the importance of getting an education, or a good lesson. I hated the idea of going to school, back in the 60's, when I was of elementary school age. I remember one of my sisters taking me to a Catholic Church for head start. I was petrified as the nuns were in long black get ups, with halibut on their heads. I was so scared, I cried for my sister and the nuns threatened to spank me, so my sister took me back home. I skipped out on head start, but this dilemma came up again, but this time I could not get out of it. I started kindergarten and hated it too, because I never felt like I fit in, and did not know I was supposed to be learning something, until I met Ms. Brooks, who saw much potential in me. My second grade teacher, Ms. Brooks, knew that I did my own work, and she saw me as smart, I believe she, also noticed that my teachers ahead of her did not have the time to spend on me getting it. After that my experience with my teachers were pretty good, and I kind of liked school and learning, even though I did not still understand to appreciate the importance of educating myself. As I went on to high school, my whole attitude changed, as I was going from adolescent to adulthood at some point, as this too was scary, because I was still trying to fit in society, and could not really appreciated the learning experience. Now, let me get to the true meat and potatoes of why educating the mind is so important. If one is not educated you have left yourself open to have to accept anything and to possibly be bamboozled, or walked all over. My understanding of an educated mind is to learn from the best teachers and your first teachers are often, your parents and then personal life experiences. Looking back, I see that not only did I learn from the school system, the streets on how to survive, as well as through relationships with other people. When we fail to educate ourselves and our children from our learning experiences, we, us, and ours, continue to fall in the realm of servitude, as we learn to become depended on a system and other people, be that as educators in marriages or in our careers, and in daily living.

Lesson: Educate yourself on anything, any topic, or situation and appreciate every person you meet good or bad. I'm sure they taught you something that will, or has carried you through life in a different light, possibly with a better understanding of how to cope with the complexity of our world.

12

Were Not That Different

It took until I was an adult, working on my career and degree at the community college, when I learned in my biology class, the difference between sex and gender. I further educated myself on this topic when I was in a Gender Studies program, where I became certified in learning about the diverse sectors of the gender spectrum. Sitting in my biology class is where I also, learned that a fetus does not form its genitals, until about three months, and until then it is often considered female. In learning this it left me thinking, where does the difference truly lie? Now, when I look at a human being, I see a person, not male or female. When we view it from a biological spectrum, we are looking at boy/girl how you're born physically, and from the gender spectrum many different looks, sexual orientation, and preferences. I guess what made it more curious is was when; I realized my child was gay. I tried to understand who my daughter was, and at times tried to force her to be who, and what I wanted her to be, based on her assigned sex. The more I learned about this topic the better understood that we are not that different, and was more accepting of my own child. Also, think on this, if we come from male and female, is it not that hard to see, that we can obtain a certain amount of attributes from both, and this does not always equate to just male or female. One of the most ridiculous things I ever heard is when a man says, "I am 100 percent man," or when a woman says this about her sex. It appears there is no such thing as 100 percent male or female, when its view from the gender spectrum, because if so, it would sort of look like this, we would have to have male on male to equal 100 percent male, but since we come from both sexes, we have a fair chance at having a lot of characteristics from both. In talking to some of my colleagues they understand this phenomenon, as in the human discipline field this is part of what we learned in educational programs, but I understand if the average Joe does not get this, because at one time, I thought like the status quo, as well on a lot of topics. Hopefully, this topic gets the mind to at least consider, how this might work, before we judge or treat people a certain way, instead work on trying to understand and build relationships with all types of people, so that we all better understand one another as we move through the journey of life.

Lesson: Building relationships through an open lens will allow for a greater understanding that we really truly are not that different.

13

Under the Sink

When I think about secrecy it really breaks my heart as a lot of behaviors form out of a lot of distorted thinking that, we grasp in our families, churches, schools, and through media, who knew hidden secrets held so much weight. The underline to this mystery is that people become so accustomed to rituals, rules, and the golden rule, really not realizing we have not tapped into other ways of looking at things. What's under the sink is a lot of anxiety around how we cope with everyday life situations. We often have come to believe that the struggle is real, when all actuality there is not struggle, rather a heavy burden of lies, and deception that we choose to feed ourselves without thinking, "Damn I too deserve to have some compassion on me." And that the truth hurts, but saves my soul and heart from the danger ahead. As a great man once said, "You can see to the corner, but not around it." I guess my point here is how many times have you beat yourself up over a "thing" that you had no control over, or maybe you did only to say I was stupid, dumb, or crazy for allowing myself to go through such a thing. It is so easy to get caught up in loving someone who maybe does not love us back, or experience ruminating thoughts that impact daily living, and yes we all have been guilty of accepting the status quo. It takes a lot of courage to build a relationship like this with the inner you, as we may have heard in spiritual messages how flesh is any enemy of flesh, which makes it hard, because this to me means, I am an enemy to me. Looking at it this way, makes one truly believe the burden is a lot heavier than it is, but the flipside to this is accepting the truth, your truth, as a good friend said to me whatever that is, as this is the true way to pull out what's under the sink and start to find who you are, as way too often we build a frame of who we are based on all of our life experiences and if we really take a look at this, we might see this does not hold to who we truly are and it can possibly take the expectations people have for us off of who we truly are, so we can acknowledge a thing, accept a thing, and know we can activate change through finding or own personal truth.

Lesson: A peaceful mind is the best relationship you can have with self through accepting what is real and true. Take a seat gather your thoughts and give yourself the pleasure of meeting you, in other words introduce you to you and the next time you look in the mirror see if you like the new you defined/designed by you.

14

Bathroom Ecstasy

This one is for me, myself and I. but, I love sharing it with my readers though. I don't know about you, but I love me some me. Growing up, I always felt like the ugly duckling. I remember a family friend telling, someone close to me that all my mother's children are cute, except this one, pointing and laughing at me. I guess what hurt the most this close relative, did not notice she was laughing with this person. I also, remember being called names that stuck, see it's not the physical hits that run the deepest, it's the emotional ones. Out of all of this, plus a few hard knocks from life, has taught me, that self-perseverance comes first, in order to love or care for anyone else to any degree. I spend time in my bathroom primping and priming, as I carry the idea that I must stay ready for whatever, as a friend once shared with me. I love how my clothes, make-up, and how my sensual being make me feel as a woman. Building this personal relationship with self has sent my self-esteem through the roof. I get more attention from the brothers and well some sisters too, because my true me at the prime of my life shines through everyday all day long. Now, I model trying to be good to others, and practice treating everyone I cross with the same respect, that I expect no matter who they are, however some make this very difficult, and it's not always strangers that give you the hardest time. Some folk, often wonder why, I wear my hair nappy, well as India Arie said, "I'm not my hair," meaning I am not defined by how I wear my hair, just because some people's hair grow down, and mines happen to grow up, does not mean mines is not just as beautiful. All this exudes through, when I am in ecstasy in my bathroom whether putting on make-up, dressing, or moisturizing my body, or in what I am wearing. More recently losing over 70ish pounds did not hurt either. I mention all this, because it was not until now, that I learned to build a relationship with me, and learned to love me for who I am, whether I lost weight or not, and I definitely stopped listening to negative messages in my own head about myself, and replaced them with more positive affirmations about loving me just the way I am, except it or not.

Lesson: Learn to love you for whom you are, and these discoveries for me came through what I call my Bathroom Ecstasies, Now what's your Ecstasy?

The Problem with Men

It hurts my heart to see my brothers skipping through life on misguided information on what it means to be a man. It seems this type of view has left many men with the idea that the definition is only what has been placed before them, without exploration of the true answer to this question. As men struggle to fit into their own personal template as a man. By now you're thinking oh writer, you mean what they learned from their daddy, well let's go deeper, because not everyone had one of those, and the one's that did may fall in this category for sure. Well in my education, I learned that the concept of what makes a man, comes out of what they learned in many areas of their life, in addition to society setting the tone, that has guided men, on how to fit into his personal template. Our society, has taught men that you're not a man if you cry early in life, so first this possibly gives young boys, or men the idea that I am less than something, if I cry, or if I am born to look like a man, then I don't have the right to feel like, or be something else. This often leaves my brothers of all races, cultures, and groups to struggle with how they view themselves. Plus drives the need to grab hold tight to what they have been taught, as far as what it takes to be a man, when all actuality there is no template. For as long as I can remember there have been all kinds of men gay, those that are not gay, strong built ones, and smaller framed ones. Question? Does any of this predict the validity of their true manhood? Let's keep it real, it's some gay brother's out there that will take out a can of whip ass on you, quick and handle their business, so this holds no weight that strength makes a man.

Furthermore, men are also taught to be leaders, head of households, work hard, and care for their families which are all adamant features, but if they fail in these areas of life, the often see themselves as weak. All of this guides a man and keeps a man from expressing who he is, and from reaching his highest heights as a human being. It seems what truly makes a man is being true to one's self, and for men to have the ability to take on good characteristics, so that he is kind and respectful and open to all the different layers to his life, so others can embrace his trueness. So sorry this one is long, but I see so many men struggle with this and not having the ability to identify what is going on with them, and this stuff too many times, shows up as power and control when barriers in life arise. In my opinion, men way to often strive to base manhood on superficial beliefs about what it takes to be a man. It does not help when my sisters call them weak, punks, and dumb asses, if they don't pay their bills. Well ladies always be prepared to pay your own bills and get into relationships for what two people can offer one another through grace and love. Come on now ladies, let's stop driving the pressure this is not the answer and no one wins this way. Yall know sista's who make statements like, "he didn't learn from his momma how to be a man", usually, when things go wrong in a relationship. Instead let's all educate ourselves; because we need our men and let's quit blaming that man's poor mama, y'all know y'all wrong for that, stop listening to male bashing songs, because just like women, they did not get a fair shake on gender either. Again, for the most part all men's struggles will remain if they themselves are not willing to break down ego and pride, so they can become cleansed of the foolish idea on what it takes to make a man, in order to be recognized as a man, and to gain the ability to express their emotions, as this type of thinking is just not emotionally healthy and keeps our men oppressed.

Lesson: We need our men and I believe change can happen, when men in our society become willing to take a second look, how they define manhood, and see the benefits of it in their relationships and with themselves, so that they can be better for the world, themselves, and their families. I don't need an Amen on this one it speaks for itself.

16

Family Dynamics

The world's model for a family is in the traditional sense, which most times looks like; man plus woman equal four or five children and a picket white fence. Our diverse world is causing us to look at this in a much different way, as a family these days can look like two men, or two women, multiple of individuals raising children and engaging in intimacy that make up a family. The meaning as definitely taken on a new course, unfortunately, not everyone has embraced this. Growing up in my family I was taught based on the traditional way of thinking about family. What this came to mean to me is, the eldest child held a lot of the families burden, and guided the younger children, much like a second mother. Now this is not in every traditional family, but it's what I saw coming up. This was cool, but the problem comes later in life, when the eldest child finds it hard to see the younger siblings as their equal in adulthood. This kind of view, can cause a lot of distorted thinking to form out of the idea this one child provided, and what it meant to me was a lot of power and control became embraced by the eldest so much, so everyone in the family-based loyalty on this one individual, what the eldest says goes from here on out. This can be good to the point the eldest becomes a good leader for self and others, but the younger children are no longer children and disrespect, power, and control seem to start to arise in many family structures, based on this type of family. And at times can take on emotional ill-treatment within the family system. The youngest in many families, don't get that same respect, and this respect is also not often given to all members, in the family unit. I think my daughter said it best, "We give and take from one another and respect

must be at the forefront of our thinking." Age differences in the family can cause a lot of displaced ideas, for what takes place in a family, as far as heritage, and respect from younger generations in the family, and how you're treated by extended family members. Now when I look at other cultures like the gay community the construction on family looks a lot different and this type of family loses a lot of relationships, because people struggle to see anything, but the traditional family as the dominant look for what a family should look like in Western cultures.

Lesson: So the next time you think of family know that anyone that has the ability to care for someone, nourish them, and provided basic needs to another can be viewed as a family and deserve the same respect no respect of age differences.

17

Front Porch Productions

I am about to take you way back. You ever wondered why people congregate on the front porch, maybe to people watch, gossip or get into heated arguments over little things, ever so often. From this it is easy to see how things formulate in mass productions and how thinking is sort of structured out of this phenomenon. Growing up in Walnut Park area of St. Louis, Missouri, I saw things take place that now days make motion pictures. I remember the first drive by shooting, while sitting on the front porch just dippy doodling along, and all of a sudden we heard pop, pop, pop, pop sound repeating itself, over and over again, only to find out the next day, that two people I could recognize from the neighborhood, were shot up and the car kept going. Now this had to be in the late 80's, during teenage years of my life. Now, it is so strange how this thing, has taken flight, and people, year after year numbed themselves to the after math of drive by shootings. Gossiping on the porch just was not the same, now that one could not even sit on the porch without thinking about the possibility of getting shot, but somehow a new survival skill set was taken on and relationships began to build to try to help our youth, but not a lot of have been able to reach them. Now let's go back and sit on the front porch again and think about how to do this. Well effective communication might be a factor, letting other brothers speak to our young men about the value of culture and the fact there is no loyalty among street dudes, and hopefully people in many communities can build greater relationships with the new generation, so that change can take place and sitting on the front porch can go back to what it used to be, where you could perhaps even sleep outside, but don't try that now.

Lesson: Charity begins at home, so if we create new relationships that open a line of communication change can perhaps take place. I try this in my encounters with youth today, so join me in winning the fight in any way possible, you might even have to put down the gossip and produce mass sources of substance, when communicating that make some effect on their young lives, as well as encourage education, goals and good success stories for this new generation, so that they can create a new look for the front porch.

18

Out the Box

It is true if you don't take possession of a thing, someone else will do it for you. I remember in the eighty's one of my sayings being "out the box" and I never spoke from a platform, where I got recognized, or got acknowledge for creating this saying. Now a day's people use it possibly, in the same way. For me I saw "out the box" as a way to say the reasoning behind something just did not fit. Funny as it may seem, this too allowed me to build good relationships with people through spoken language, as they started saying "out the box" too, now I felt like when this saying resurfaced, I had already coined it in my world. I don't know if I would have gotten paid, but maybe recognized in the Webster for creating it, while this sounds condescending, for me, I was able to speak a

word and relate it to something and people caught on to it. Think on this, we can use this same assumption about how to be creative, or in making something, or possibly building something, or even in teaching someone something that gives them purpose and meaning in life, while building great relationship people, and you might even ended up getting paid for your idea, if it catches like "out the box" surely did.

Lesson: Make sure you own what you feel you created, or someone else will take your idea and use it for their good, even though it might seem ridiculous, remember to patent, get in black and white things you desire to take ownership of to make a better you. Hopefully, lesson is received, at times it takes several times to hear this, or when you take your idea to the grave and someone lives vicariously through you, at any rate own it if it's yours no matter what your desire may be.

19

Whose Really Insane

I am so grateful to be a Social Worker, and to have worked and met people who have acknowledged they need help for their mental health. So many times people walk through life with low self-esteem and are not able to equate this to depression or feel angry without knowing people really take medications for anxiety, which is what anger comes out of and as a result what we see is a lot of people, who are on edge that can easily go from zero to one hundred, and this produces behaviors that can lead to lethal endings for some, like where does all that energy come from to commit mass killings, or to engaged in domestic abuse or the energy to just punch the guy out who stole your parking spot as the department store. What I think is so amazing is the workers who find a way every day to face these types of people to get them help, before they make it to those points. They do this, by teaching coping skills against an angry heart, or by addressing real issues of low self-esteem and what this may stem from. Addressing your mental health is probably the last thing on a person's mind who thinks they are sanely OK, even in a world like the one we live in. As a Social Worker, I don't do too much judging people, but rather diagnosing their behavior based on DSM 5, I don't' mean to talk over your heads, but people as a great friend favorite saying to me is, the definition of Insanity, is to do the same thing over and over and expect a different result, is what people often do including myself only to arrive at the same answer. Now for me, I began taking better care of my mental health, when I started working with the mental health population, plus I learned a few things about me, and how to tap into my emotions, as well as change behavior after learning how to cope with distorted thinking patterns I picked up along the way in life.

Lesson: People struggle or have not realized the need, to take care of their mental health, and often believe they are taking care of mental health when they exercise or go to the gym, however these are not one in the same. For a full life it would benefit one to take care of their physical, mental, spiritual health, and if need be their sexual health, for a better chance at a long healthy life. For you, young ones it's not time to take care of your sexual health if you're not of age. Be wise my people and look holistically at your overall well-being. It is to be acknowledged, when one can be true to self and know when the need for help is through addressing one's mental health, so the connection to mind body and soul can take place.

Dedicated to my dear friend Fire, Educator of Health and Wellness.

20

Mouth Full of Laughter

U hmm, where do I start the importance of laughter is so rich. I have been a jokester all of my life. I remember coming up, my sister whose closes to my age, grew up laughing at any and everything. We used to even do what we called "laugh at a laugh". My dad would yell up the stairs on a school night, "stop all that laughing and go to bed!" I will swear by laughter and the fact that it is also a great way to cope with life stressors. I have learned in life that I came across the greatest friends to this day through sharing laughter, One friend in particular is someone whom I respect as confidants and this person and I will take to the grave secrets we shared, real talk, and yes of course girl talk, and a lot of laughter. If the world could just burst out in one big old ball of laughter, we might all just be able to overcome a lot of the stress that has been place on our world. Through laughter, I have built great friendships and relationships, be that with my relatives, friends, or co-workers. Recently, I have grown very close to my dear friend and sister, who she and I call ourselves Gayle and she is my Oprah. We share great stories and she gets how I think. I am so grateful to be so blessed to have met her in the way that I did, and only she knows.

Lesson: Friends come and go for a season, but a friend that turns out to be a true sister to you will always be by your side, and I am so grateful that a relationship was built, when two great minds were put in the same room and these two started learning together, as well as sharing life experiences, and who thinks a lot alike on many levels, and we often experience this through a mouth of full laughter.

Lesson Received.
To my dear friend,
Radiance, the Pioneer Woman and Gardner.

Be blessed and thanks for having an open heart and mind, in taking your valuable time to read this amusing, interesting book about my guiding principles of life. It does not hurt; there is a little humor in the book too. It also, capture parts of you that you may have struggled to speak about and where you are tired of the hush hush on these types of issues as well.

Notes Page 1

Notes Page 2

Notes Page 3

Notes Page 4

This book is an eye opener to a lot of people who question a lot of things about their lives, value systems around religion, the trauma experience, and a host of other life experiences, where outcomes formed lasting relationships with self, and others be that good or bad. It is the writer's hope that this book touches lives in a way, we all learn to love and respect one another for, who we are, and just for being a human being. Hopefully, the life experiences in this book touches those that struggle with the complexity of the world, in which we all live, as this is my reason for writing a book of this nature.

I Love You All
Susan Cook "Songbird"

"One who is willing to pass on service to mankind through love and dedication from those who have done the same for her through the wings of a songbird, so you too, can soar through life with much more ease."

SUSAN M. COOK, is a MSW-Social Worker, CADC (Certified Alcohol and Drug Counselor), working for mankind for over twenty years. Susan was born and raised in inner city located in Saint Louis, Missouri. Susan understands the challenge of being a single mother, misguided youth, youngest girl of eight children, and daughter of parents, who were faced with poverty and strife, and behind the scenes taboos and secrecy followed her life in many experiences. Susan would like her work to help individuals, and families change generations through openness of learning life lessons to overcome adversity. Susan, herself returned to school as a non-traditional student at the age of 38, and she completed her Bachelors Program in Saint Louis, Missouri at the University of Missouri – St. Louis campus, and a one year track, Master's Program at the University of Central Florida, with two Certifications one in Gender Studies, and a Military Certificate, that certifies her to work with military families in particular, due to six of her seven uncles serving in the military, and a host of other family and friends. Susan's Inspiration for writing this book, came out of a conversation with her mentor Mr. George Fewquay. After writing it, she really started to realize how this book could help others, and how it became a way for her to pay it forward, as so many had done for her. It is the writer's request to invite readers to look forward to future writings that will transition out of the birth of The Growth of Axiom.

Printed in the United States
By Bookmasters